EVERYTHING IS CONNECTED

REIMAGINING THE WORLD ONE POSTCARD AT A TIME

KERI SMITH

A Perigee Book

P9-CQZ-520

A PERIGEE BOOK
Published by the Penguin Group
Penguin Group (USA) Inc.
375 Hudson Street, New York, New York 10014, USA

USA | Canada | UK | Ireland | Australia | New Zealand | India | South Africa | China

Penguin Books Ltd., Registered Offices: 80 Strand, London WC2R 0RL, England
For more information about the Penguin Group, visit penguin.com.

EVERYTHING IS CONNECTED

Copyright © 2013 by Keri Smith
All rights reserved. No part of this book may be reproduced, scanned, or distributed in
any printed or electronic form without permission. Please do not participate in or encourage piracy of
copyrighted materials in violation of the author's rights. Purchase only authorized editions.
PERIGEE is a registered trademark of Penguin Group (USA) Inc.
The "P" design is a trademark belonging to Penguin Group (USA) Inc.

ISBN: 978-0-399-16518-4

First edition: October 2013

PRINTED IN CHINA

10 9 8 7 6 5 4 3 2 1

Art and design by Keri Smith

PEARSON

ALWAYS LEARNING

DOCUMENT Things YOU _SEE_ ON  YOUR way to  Mail this POSTCARD.

_____

_____

_____

_____

_____

_____

_____

_____

_____

PLACE
STAMP
HERE

IMAGE © 2013, EVERYTHING IS CONNECTED BY KERI SMITH

This card seems to be asking you to take a journey of sorts. You will use it to explore the world via aimless wandering.

• Roll the die.
• Take five steps in the direction indicated.
• Continue rolling the die. Document your movement.

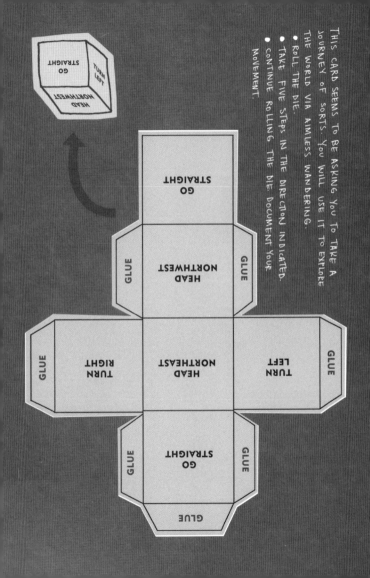

GO STRAIGHT

HEAD NORTHWEST

GLUE

GLUE

TURN RIGHT

HEAD NORTHEAST

TURN LEFT

GLUE

GLUE

GLUE

GO STRAIGHT

GLUE

GLUE

GLUE

GO STRAIGHT

TURN LEFT

HEAD NORTHWEST

PLACE STAMP HERE

IMAGE © 2013, EVERYTHING IS CONNECTED BY KERI SMITH

Random Experience Generator

Plate 46

Leave this postcard in a public place.	Send this to someone you haven't seen in a long time.	Write a letter using a pseudonym.
Write a letter that only makes sense to the recipient.	Write a letter using no "E's."	Write a letter about what you did today.
Send this postcard to a former teacher.	Leave this postcard in a tree.	Write a letter giving the recipient a challenging task.
Send this postcard to someone in your best friend's family.	Write a letter using your wrong hand.	Send this postcard to a foreign country.

PLACE
STAMP
HERE

IMAGE © 2013, EVERYTHING IS CONNECTED BY KERI SMITH

YOU HAVE IMMENSE POWERS.
REPURPOSE THIS EMPTY LOT.
TRANSFORM IT INTO SOMETHING
THAT WILL HELP THE PLANET.

PLACE STAMP HERE

IMAGE © 2013, EVERYTHING IS CONNECTED BY KERI SMITH

INCONVENIENCE

TAKE THIS POSTCARD
EVERYWHERE YOU GO FOR
ONE WEEK. YOU MUST
PLACE IT IN FULL VIEW
AT ALL TIMES.

PLACE
STAMP
HERE

IMAGE © 2013, EVERYTHING IS CONNECTED BY KERI SMITH

SECRET IDENTITY PROFILE
(WHO WOULD YOU LIKE TO BE?)

NAME:
PLACE OF BIRTH:
DATE OF BIRTH:
PROFESSION:
LIKES:

DISLIKES:

LOCATION:

LIFESTYLE SYNOPSIS (DAILY ACTIVITIES):

PERSONAL HABITS:

HOBBIES:

GROUPS & ASSOCIATIONS:

SOCIAL LIFE:

PLACE STAMP HERE

IMAGE © 2013, EVERYTHING IS CONNECTED BY KERI SMITH

DEAR FRIEND,

THIS IS A CHAIN LETTER.
IT'S ONLY PURPOSE IS TO SEE
HOW FAR IT CAN GO.
ADD YOUR NAME AND LOCATION
TO THE BOTTOM OF THE LIST.
THEN SEND THE LETTER TO
ONE FRIEND.

ORIGINATOR: _ _ _ _ _ _ _ _ _ _ _ _
_ _ _ _ _ _ _ _ _ _ _ _
_ _ _ _ _ _ _ _ _ _ _ _

_ _

_ _

_ _

PLACE
STAMP
HERE

IMAGE © 2013, EVERYTHING IS CONNECTED BY KERI SMITH

THIS IS YOUR VERY OWN PLANET.
YOU MUST ADD THINGS TO IT TO MAKE
IT FLOURISH.
- CREATE A LEGEND WITH SYMBOLS
  TO ADD BUILDINGS, PEOPLE, AND THINGS
  FROM YOUR IMAGINATION.
- DESCRIBE THE WEATHER AND THE INHABITANTS;
  ADD ROADS, ETC.

PLACE
STAMP
HERE

IMAGE © 2013, EVERYTHING IS CONNECTED BY KERI SMITH

ITINERARY.

- GO TO THE CLOSEST PARK.

- SPEND 10 MINUTES LOOKING AT THE SKY. WHAT DO YOU SEE?

- DOCUMENT YOURSELF STANDING UNDER A TREE (PHOTO, DRAWING, ETC.).

- ARRANGE SOMETHING YOU FIND INTO A CIRCLE (LEAVES, STONES, ETC.).

- LIST THE NUMBER OF PEOPLE YOU SEE.

- LEAVE SOMETHING OF YOURS IN A SECRET LOCATION.

PLACE STAMP HERE

IMAGE © 2013, EVERYTHING IS CONNECTED BY KERI SMITH

THIS DAY WILL NEVER HAPPEN AGAIN

(INSERT DATE HERE)

PLACE STAMP HERE

IMAGE © 2013, EVERYTHING IS CONNECTED BY KERI SMITH

THIS IS A **PORTABLE HOLE/PORTAL.**

MAKES THINGS DISAPPEAR AT WILL.

- CUT OUT.
- AFFIX THE HOLE TO ANY SURFACE.
- USE.

PLACE
STAMP
HERE

IMAGE © 2013, EVERYTHING IS CONNECTED BY KERI SMITH

CARVE SOMETHING ONTO THIS TREE.

PLACE
STAMP
HERE

IMAGE © 2013, EVERYTHING IS CONNECTED BY KERI SMITH

THIS POSTCARD IS A SCULPTURE

USE THIS CARD TO CREATE A THREE-DIMENSIONAL OBJECT. EXHIBIT IT SOMEWHERE.

PLACE STAMP HERE

IMAGE © 2013, EVERYTHING IS CONNECTED BY KERI SMITH

THIS IS A
PUBLIC SPACE.
INVITE PEOPLE TO ADD SOMETHING
TO THIS PAGE.

PLACE STAMP HERE

IMAGE © 2013, EVERYTHING IS CONNECTED BY KERI SMITH

DO NOT STICK ANYTHING HERE. DO NOT SCRIBBLE ON THIS POSTCARD. DO NOT COVER UP THIS TYPE. DO NOT TOUCH THIS POSTCARD WITH DIRTY HANDS. DO NOT READ THIS POSTCARD WHILE EATING. DO NOT WALK ON THIS POSTCARD WITH YOUR SHOES. DO NOT RUB THIS POSTCARD WITH DIRT. DO NOT FOLD DOWN THE CORNERS OF THIS POSTCARD. DO NOT WRITE NOTES TO YOUR FRIENDS HERE. DO NOT TEAR THIS POSTCARD. DO NOT GET THIS POSTCARD WET. DO NOT LET A FRIEND WRITE ON THIS POSTCARD. DO NOT TRY TO COVER UP THIS POSTCARD. BREAK THE RULES.

PLACE STAMP HERE

IMAGE © 2013, EVERYTHING IS CONNECTED BY KERI SMITH

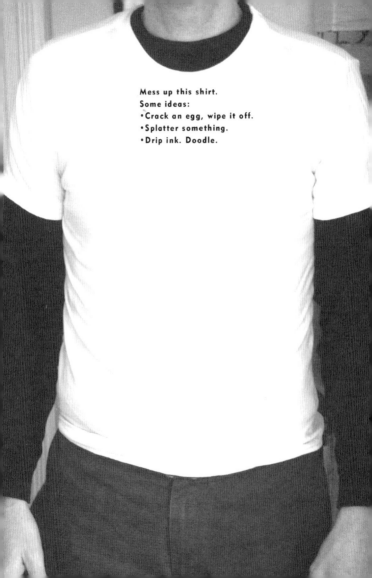

Mess up this shirt.
Some ideas:
• Crack an egg, wipe it off.
• Splatter something.
• Drip ink. Doodle.

PLACE STAMP HERE

IMAGE © 2013, EVERYTHING IS CONNECTED BY KERI SMITH

Create a mess here with a friend while having lunch together.

PLACE STAMP HERE

IMAGE © 2013, EVERYTHING IS CONNECTED BY KERI SMITH

HIDE THIS POSTCARD
IN YOUR NEIGHBOR'S
YARD.

PLACE STAMP HERE

IMAGE © 2013, EVERYTHING IS CONNECTED BY KERI SMITH

COLLECT FRUIT STICKERS HERE.

PLACE STAMP HERE

IMAGE © 2013, EVERYTHING IS CONNECTED BY KERI SMITH

CONVERSATION STARTER BADGE

1. CUT ALONG DOTTED LINE.
2. AFFIX TO CLOTHING.

PLACE STAMP HERE

IMAGE © 2013, EVERYTHING IS CONNECTED BY KERI SMITH

MERIT BADGES
for STRANGERS

THANK YOU FOR BEING YOURSELF

I really LIKE WHAT YOU'RE DOING.

YOU LOOK REALLY GOOD TODAY.

YOU MADE IT! THIS FAR.

PLACE STAMP HERE

IMAGE © 2013, EVERYTHING IS CONNECTED BY KERI SMITH

COUPONS

THIS COUPON ENTITLES THE USER TO DO THE OPPOSITE OF WHAT S/HE PLANNED FOR THE DAY.

THIS COUPON ENTITLES THE USER TO ONE DAY TO DO SOME RANDOM WANDERING.

THIS COUPON ENTITLES THE USER TO TURN THEIR WORLD INTO AN IMAGINED REALITY FOR A FEW HOURS.

THIS COUPON ENTITLES THE USER TO DO SOMETHING COMPLETELY OUT OF CHARACTER.

THIS COUPON ENTITLES THE USER TO MOVE AS SLOWLY AS POSSIBLE WHILE GOING ABOUT THEIR EVERYDAY ACTIVITIES.

THIS COUPON ENTITLES THE USER TO WEAR A DISGUISE.

THIS COUPON ENTITLES THE USER TO SOME DEEP BREATHS.

THIS COUPON ENTITLES THE USER TO A DIFFERENT PERSPECTIVE.

PLACE STAMP HERE

IMAGE © 2013, EVERYTHING IS CONNECTED BY KERI SMITH

SEE HOW MANY TIMES
YOU CAN MAIL THIS
POSTCARD BACK AND
FORTH TO A FRIEND.

WRITE VERY SMALL SO YOU CAN
ADD TO IT EACH TIME.

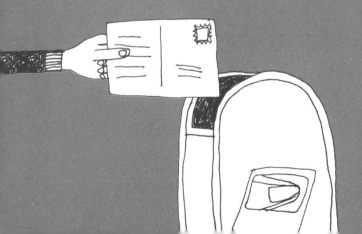

PLACE STAMP HERE

IMAGE © 2013, EVERYTHING IS CONNECTED BY KERI SMITH

THIS POSTCARD HAS MAGIC POWERS.

WHAT WOULD YOU LIKE IT TO DO?

PLACE STAMP HERE

IMAGE © 2013, EVERYTHING IS CONNECTED BY KERI SMITH

CUT OUT

VERY IMPORTANT PERSON

DIRECTIONS:
- CUT OUT SQUARE.
- HOLD UP FRAME AND PHOTOGRAPH PEOPLE.
- SEND THEM A COPY.

PLACE STAMP HERE

IMAGE © 2013, EVERYTHING IS CONNECTED BY KERI SMITH

USE THIS SPACE

TO WRITE SOMETHING REALLY
IMPORTANT AND SECRET
(SOMETHING YOU'VE NEVER TOLD
ANYONE ELSE). CHOOSE ONE
OF THE FOLLOWING OPTIONS:

- DESTROY THE CARD BEFORE
  ANYONE SEES IT.

- MAIL IT TO A STRANGER.

PLACE STAMP HERE

IMAGE © 2013, EVERYTHING IS CONNECTED BY KERI SMITH

I THINK WE SHOULD MEET IN PERSON, INSTEAD OF CONNECTING ON

facebook.

DATE: _____

TIME: _____

PLACE STAMP HERE

IMAGE © 2013, EVERYTHING IS CONNECTED BY KERI SMITH

DO SOMETHING INTERESTING WITH **THESE** <u>HOLES</u>.

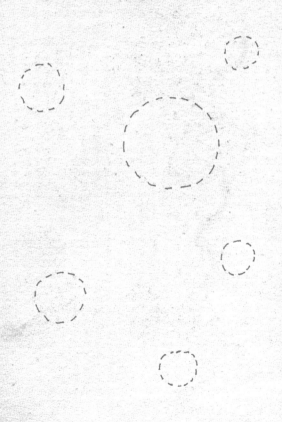

PLACE STAMP HERE

IMAGE © 2013, EVERYTHING IS CONNECTED BY KERI SMITH

THIS IS A PORTRAIT OF ME AS A SUPERHERO.

THIS IS A PORTRAIT OF YOU AS A BAD GUY.

PLACE STAMP HERE

IMAGE © 2013, EVERYTHING IS CONNECTED BY KERI SMITH

THIS IS A GAME.

PLAYERS TAKE TURNS PLACING THIS POSTCARD
IN A DIFFERENT LOCATION FOR EACH ROUND.

THERE ARE FIVE ROUNDS. IN EACH ROUND
PLAYERS TAKE TURNS RETRIEVING THIS POSTCARD
ACCORDING TO THE REQUIREMENTS ON THE LIST.

OPTIONAL: TIME EACH ROUND. GIVE EACH PLAYER
TWO MINUTES.

CREATE FIVE MORE REQUIREMENTS (ROUNDS).

ROUND ONE: RETRIEVE THIS POSTCARD
WITH EYES SHUT.

ROUND TWO: RETRIEVE THIS POSTCARD
WITH NO HANDS.

ROUND THREE: CONVINCE A THIRD PARTY TO
RETRIEVE THIS POSTCARD
FOR YOU.

ROUND FOUR: RETRIEVE THIS POSTCARD
WHILE STANDING ON ONE LEG.

ROUND FIVE: RETRIEVE THIS POSTCARD
USING A TOOL OR UTENSIL.

PLACE STAMP HERE

IMAGE © 2013, EVERYTHING IS CONNECTED BY KERI SMITH

THIS IS A **LOST TREASURE**.

- FIND A GOOD HIDING SPOT FOR THIS POSTCARD.
- CREATE A "TREASURE MAP."
- GIVE THE MAP TO A FRIEND AND INSTRUCT THEM TO FIND THE TREASURE.

PLACE STAMP HERE

IMAGE © 2013, EVERYTHING IS CONNECTED BY KERI SMITH

EXPERIENCE MAP
MAP PLACES ASSOCIATED
WITH YOUR MEMORIES.

HAND MAP

DOG
CHEEK
TEETH
SAND
BOOGER
SHELL

GLUE
PAPER
GLASS
THORN

WOOD
HAIR

LIPS
PHONE
FOOD
NEWSPAPER
SHEETS

HAMMER
GRASS
FLOOR

TREE
ROPE
BALLOON

STEERING WHEEL
PAINT
FUR
WOOL

ZIPPER
PLASTIC
BAG
RAIN
DOOR KNOB

SNOW
BUG

RING

KEYS BOOK
FLOWER NOSE
STEM
BABY
BUTTON
FORK
CLOTH
MUG DROOL
VOMIT
BIRD
MITTENS GRAVEL
STONE

YOUR   HAND   WAY
SWING   LICHEN BACK
PEBBLES   WIRE   DIRT
WATER   BAG
EGG METAL
FEATHER CLAY POO
BASEBALL
PLASTIC CARPET
POISON IVY MUSHROOM MEAT
URINE   BLOOD COBWEB PAVEMENT
FRUIT JUICE LEATHER
CACTUS
NECK
FINGERS

PLACE STAMP HERE

IMAGE © 2013, EVERYTHING IS CONNECTED BY KERI SMITH

DETAILED EVENTS OF A DAY IN THE FUTURE.

_____

_____

_____

_____

_____

_____

_____

_____

_____

_____

_____

_____

PLACE STAMP HERE

IMAGE © 2013, EVERYTHING IS CONNECTED BY KERI SMITH

POST CARD
OF RANDOM
THOUGHTS.

PLACE STAMP HERE

IMAGE © 2013, EVERYTHING IS CONNECTED BY KERI SMITH

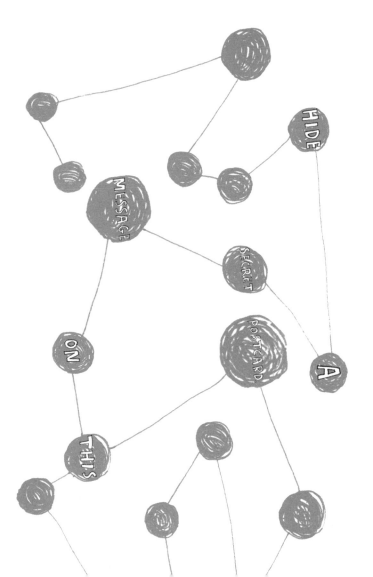

PLACE STAMP HERE

IMAGE © 2013, EVERYTHING IS CONNECTED BY KERI SMITH

THIS POSTCARD IS A SIGN.
WHAT DO YOU WANT IT TO SAY?

PLACE STAMP HERE

IMAGE © 2013, EVERYTHING IS CONNECTED BY KERI SMITH

FORTUNE TELLER
- CUT OUT SQUARES.
- ASK A YES OR NO QUESTION.
- CLOSE EYES AND PICK A
  SQUARE FOR YOUR ANSWER.

YES

NO

MAYBE

THIS IS A
MYSTERY

TRY
AGAIN

PLACE STAMP HERE

IMAGE © 2013, EVERYTHING IS CONNECTED BY KERI SMITH

IDEA FORMULATION GENERATOR

- IN BOX ONE MAKE A LIST OF THINGS FOUND IN NATURE.

- IN BOX TWO MAKE A LIST OF OBJECTS YOU USE EVERY DAY.

- IN BOX THREE MAKE A LIST OF WORDS YOU LIKE.

- PICK ONE ITEM FROM EACH LIST AND COMBINE THEM TO COME UP WITH AN IDEA FOR A NEW PRODUCT OR CONCEPT.

PLACE STAMP HERE

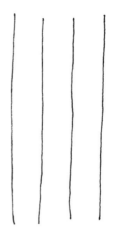

IMAGE © 2013, EVERYTHING IS CONNECTED BY KERI SMITH

ACTION
POSTCARD
COME UP WITH AN
INTERESTING WAY TO
MAKE THIS CARD MOVE.

PLACE STAMP HERE

IMAGE © 2013, EVERYTHING IS CONNECTED BY KERI SMITH

RANDOM LETTER

Get a dictionary.
• The first word of your letter must be chosen from page 48.
• The fifth word of your letter must be chosen from page 10.
• The twelfth word of your letter must be chosen from page 100.
• The eighteenth word of your letter must be chosen from page 25.

PLACE STAMP HERE

IMAGE © 2013, EVERYTHING IS CONNECTED BY KERI SMITH

VOYAGE

- FOLD THIS POSTCARD INTO A BOAT.
- FIND A BODY OF WATER.
- SET IT ADRIFT.

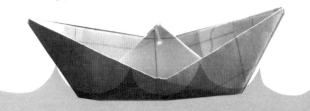

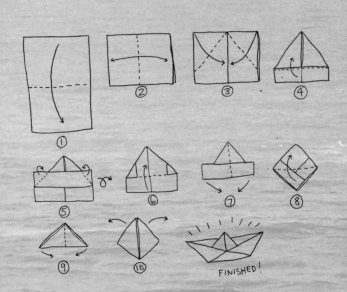

① ② ③ ④ ⑤ ⑥ ⑦ ⑧ ⑨ ⑩ FINISHED!

PLACE
STAMP
HERE

IMAGE © 2013, EVERYTHING IS CONNECTED BY KERI SMITH

SMUDGE LOG

Create random smudges in each of these squares while you are going about your day.
- Experiment with different substances.
- Document where and when each smudge was made.

DATE	DATE	DATE	DATE
TIME	TIME	TIME	TIME
LOCATION	LOCATION	LOCATION	LOCATION
DATE	DATE	DATE	DATE
TIME	TIME	TIME	TIME
LOCATION	LOCATION	LOCATION	LOCATION
DATE	DATE	DATE	DATE
TIME	TIME	TIME	TIME
LOCATION	LOCATION	LOCATION	LOCATION
DATE	DATE	DATE	DATE
TIME	TIME	TIME	TIME
LOCATION	LOCATION	LOCATION	LOCATION

PLACE STAMP HERE

IMAGE © 2013, EVERYTHING IS CONNECTED BY KERI SMITH

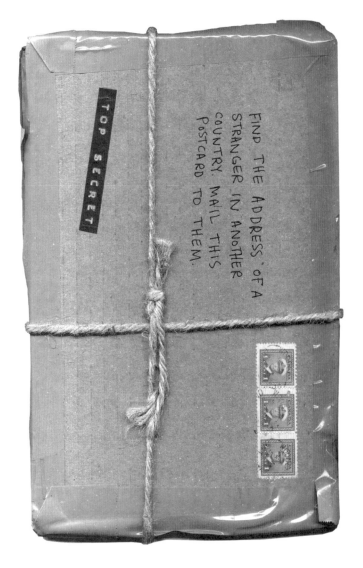

FIND THE ADDRESS OF A STRANGER IN ANOTHER COUNTRY. MAIL THIS POSTCARD TO THEM.

TOP SECRET

PLACE STAMP HERE

IMAGE © 2013, EVERYTHING IS CONNECTED BY KERI SMITH

WRITE ABOUT WHAT YOU
DID TODAY.

SEND THIS TO SOMEONE
YOU DON'T KNOW VERY
WELL.

PLACE STAMP HERE

IMAGE © 2013, EVERYTHING IS CONNECTED BY KERI SMITH

USE THIS POSTCARD
TO COVER UP OR
REPLACE SOMETHING
YOU DON'T LIKE ON
A BULLETIN BOARD.

PLACE STAMP HERE

IMAGE © 2013, EVERYTHING IS CONNECTED BY KERI SMITH

TIME TRAVEL DEVICE

- THINK OF A TIME AND PLACE YOU WOULD LIKE TO REVISIT. ENTER IT ON THE SCREEN BELOW.

- MAKE DETAILED NOTES INCLUDING EVERYTHING YOU CAN REMEMBER ABOUT THAT TIME—COLORS, SMELLS, LIGHT, TIME OF DAY, NAMES, SPACE.

- ALTERNATE: WRITE ABOUT A FUTURE TIME AND PLACE USING YOUR IMAGINATION.

PLACE STAMP HERE

IMAGE © 2013, EVERYTHING IS CONNECTED BY KERI SMITH

SEND THIS POSTCARD TO SOMEONE WITH THE SAME NAME AS YOU.

KERI SMITH
LOCATION: CHELAN, WASHINGTON
DATE: JULY 21, 2003
INFO: HAS A LARGE FAMILY &
LOTS OF KIDS. GOES ON LOTS OF FAMILY
VACATIONS.

KERI SMITH
LOCATION: SOUTHERN CALIFORNIA
WORKS AT LOMA LINDA UNIVERSITY
INFO: ADMISSIONS OFFICER, SCHOOL OF
DENTISTRY

KERI SMITH
LOCATION: OKLAHOMA
UNIVERSITY
INFO: CHEERLEADER
DATE: 2006

KERI SMITH
LOCATION: KENNETT, MISSOURI
INFO: NEW BRANCH MANAGER
OF AMERICAN HOMECARE DATE: FEB 17, 2007

KERI SMITH
LOCATION: CHAROLOTTE, NC
INFO: STUDENT ASSIST.
UNIVERSITY OF NC

KERI SMITH
LOCATION: UNKNOWN
INFO: WORKS FOR
BCAA TRAVEL

PLACE STAMP HERE

IMAGE © 2013, EVERYTHING IS CONNECTED BY KERI SMITH

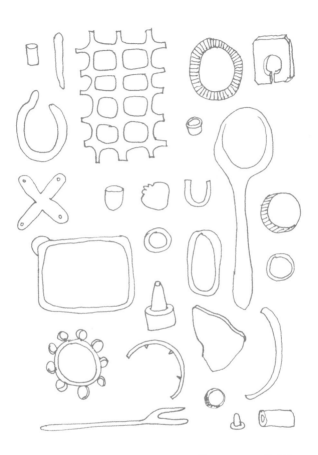

SEND A SMALL COLLECTION OF FOUND FLAT THINGS
TO A FRIEND. FIGURE OUT A WAY TO ATTACH THEM
TO THIS POSTCARD, OR USE AN ENVELOPE. ASK THEM
TO DO SOMETHING WITH THE COLLECTION AND SEND
IT BACK TO YOU.

PLACE STAMP HERE

IMAGE © 2013, EVERYTHING IS CONNECTED BY KERI SMITH

CURRENCY

USE THIS MONEY TO BEGIN YOUR
OWN ECONOMY AND BARTER SYSTEM.

TRADE THIS POSTCARD FOR ANOTHER ITEM
OF EQUAL OR GREATER VALUE.

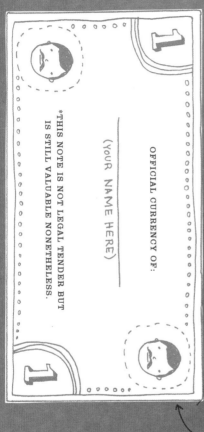

OFFICIAL CURRENCY OF:

(YOUR NAME HERE)

*THIS NOTE IS NOT LEGAL TENDER BUT
IS STILL VALUABLE NONETHELESS.

PLACE A PHOTO
OF YOURSELF HERE

PLACE STAMP HERE

IMAGE © 2013, EVERYTHING IS CONNECTED BY KERI SMITH

THE FOREST

THIS IS A FOREST TO GET LOST IN. YOU MIGHT WANT TO THINK OF IT AS A MINI-RETREAT, OR A PLACE TO SIT AND THINK. YOU MIGHT WANT TO DREAM ABOUT BUILDING A CABIN HERE, OR JUST IMAGINE TAKING A WALK WITH SOMEONE YOU LOVE. ENJOY THE SMELLS AND THE FEELING OF YOUR FEET ON THE EARTH. OH, THE SUN JUST CAME OUT! WHAT SOUNDS CAN YOU HEAR NOW?

PLACE
STAMP
HERE

IMAGE © 2013, EVERYTHING IS CONNECTED BY KERI SMITH